THINKING TOGETHER

Primary Assemblies

by

Patricia J Hunt

MOORLEY'S Print & Publishing

© Copyright 1997

All rights reserved. No part of this publication may be
reproduced, stored in a retrieval system, or
transmitted, in any form or by any means,
electronic, mechanical, photocopying, recording
or otherwise, without the prior
written permission of the publishers.

British Library Cataloguing in Publication Data.
A catalogue record for this book is available
from the British Library.

ISBN 0 86071 462 4

MOORLEY'S Print & Publishing

23 Park Rd., Ilkeston, Derbys DE7 5DA
Tel/Fax: (0115) 932 0643

CONTENTS

Page

Section A: Mainly for Infants
Useful Pets 7
Little Things Count 11
Friendly Hands 13
Riches 15
In The Beginning, God 17
Good News (The Bible) 19
Keeping Your Temper 23
Music 25
For The Glory Of God 27

Section B: Mainly for Juniors
Determination (Mary Jones) 29
Bravery (Bishop Patteson) 31
Helping Blindness Through Blindness (Fr. Jackson) 33
Aiming High (Henry Martyn) 35
Each One Teach One (Frank Laubach) 37
Fighting Disease (Father Damien) 39
Telling the Truth (Micaiah) 41
Being Sincere 45
What Goes Inside 47
The Three Monkeys (See, Hear and Speak no Evil) 49
Giving 51
Handicaps (Showing Concern) 53
Growing in Prayer 55
Isaac Watts 57
Being Lukewarm 59
Hands Off! 61
Belonging 63
What You Are Really Like 65
Symbols in Road Signs 67
I Believe 69
Quarrels and Arguments 71

Section A: Mainly for Infants

USEFUL PETS

Ask the children who has a pet at home. Ask for a show of hands as to who has a rabbit, a hamster, a canary, a kitten, a puppy, etc. If the school has any animals, these could be on display during the Assembly.

What sort of things do you notice about your pet? The way it behaves? *(A few children could give examples).* The way it is made. Have you ever looked at your pet carefully to see how wonderfully and perfectly it is made? The kitten's beautifully soft fur which you love to stroke, the tiny feathers on a canary or other small bird, the wonderfully-formed claws, the puppy's eyes as it looks up at you, etc. *(Children may give other examples).*

None of us could make any of these things. We could not even make a tiny feather in a small bird's wing. Only God can make these things so perfectly and so beautifully.

Why do you keep your pet? Because you love it? That is probably the answer which most of us would give. But some pets are kept because they are useful too. Ask for suggested uses - e.g. guard dog to keep the home safe, hens to lay eggs, donkey to give rides.

Perhaps the most useful pets are those special dogs which are Guide Dogs for blind people. Do you know anyone who is blind? *(Ensure that very small children know that this means not being able to see).* Do you know anyone who has a Guide Dog? *(Show picture, if possible, of a guide dog leading a blind person).*

Can you imagine what it would be like to be blind? *(Suggest one or two children are blindfolded and asked to cross the room).* If you were like that all the time, you would probably never dare to go anywhere on your own.

The dog and its owner have to have quite a long and special training so that they may get quite used to one another. The blind person has to learn to trust the dog, and the dog has to know when it is safe for the blind person to cross the road and to walk round obstacles in safety. The dog always leads the blind person round anything which is in the way - a pillar box, someone standing with a pram, a workman's hut, and so on. When it is time to cross the road, the dog will stay on the edge of the kerb until it can see that the road is clear to cross. *(Two children might act this, with one smaller child being the dog, and the other, blindfolded, being the blind person)*. One blind lady said that she felt her dog was really trustworthy when it was able to take her on to a railway platform; she had been terrified of going on one for fear that she might fall over the edge on to the line.

It is suggested that, if the school does not already collect, that a collection be started of silver foil, milk bottle tops, etc., to be given to the Guide Dogs for the Blind Association. (Headquarters address: Hillfields, Burghfield, Reading, Berks. RG7 3YG *(or your nearest collector)*.

<u>A Prayer</u>

Thank you God, our Heavenly Father, for our pets and for all the pleasure and fun which they give to us. Thank You for the wonderful way in which You have made them - their soft fur which is lovely to stroke, their appealing eyes, the perfect way in which you have made every tiny part of them.

Thank You especially for guide dogs which help people who are blind. May we always be kind to all animals and to all the creatures which You have so perfectly and wonderfully made.

<u>Hymns</u> - Who Put The Colours In The Rainbow?

All Things Bright and Beautiful (draw attention to the last verse - 'He gave us <u>eyes</u> to see them.....')

(For Older Children)

When God made the world He made all things with a purpose; many things are made to do good, others are to beautify the world, others have specific uses.

In no way was creation wasteful or useless. If we think something is useless, we are probably looking at it in the wrong way. It is in man's mis-use of things, people and creatures, that the causes of unhappiness, misery and sin are found. We are stewards of God's bounty, and we must think about the right uses of all the wonderful things God has given us.

LITTLE THINGS COUNT

Susan was very fond of gardening, and she had her own little patch in her father's big garden. One year she decided she wasn't going to bother with it any more.

'Why not?' asked her father. 'You like gardening.'

'Yes, but my little bit seems so unimportant with all the things which you sow. No-one would miss my few flowers if I didn't grow any.'

But that is where Susan was wrong. It is the little things which count. When Jesus came to earth to show us what God is like, He began His Kingdom with twelve men. Only twelve men - who were to go out and spread the good news of Jesus to the whole world. (Matthew 28. 19-20). It must have seemed an impossible task for them. Yet they set about it with God's help; and the result was that there are millions of Christians all over the world now - nearly two thousand years later. If those twelve men had thought that their little effort didn't count, what would have happened? Would there be any Christians today?

Jesus told a story to illustrate this. He said that a mustard seed, the tiniest of seeds, can grow until it becomes the biggest of plants - so big that birds come and make their nests in its branches. (Read Matthew 13. 31-32). That, Jesus said, is what the growth of God's Kingdom is like. It may not be noisy and showy - the mustard seed was not, - but all the time it is there, growing quietly and getting bigger and bigger.

Just imagine what would have happened if Susan had neglected her garden and had done nothing to cultivate it, even though the patch was small. It would soon have become full of weeds, which would blow all over the place, so spoiling father's garden too. It would have become an utterly useless, wasteful piece of ground.

Little things often don't look very impressive to the rest of the world, but they can be very important. Sometimes it takes only one person, with the right idea, to start a whole new movement. It may be someone very ordinary - or perhaps a tiny group of people, who can start something really big. But if they were to think, 'there are only two or three of us; nobody will be very interested, so let us give up the whole idea,' then nothing would get done, for their idea would not start and have a chance to grow.

Susan and her tiny garden; Jesus and His twelve disciples; the tiny mustard seed; all three examples of how things can grow from a very small beginning. You never know what the result of a small piece of work, or a single idea, will be. At the time, it will probably seem quite unimportant and nobody may seem interested; but with the power of God behind it, and the determination of the person who started it, the piece of work or the idea could grow beyond all expectation. But if we don't even start it off, if we give up right at the beginning, then it can never grow at all.

How will other people judge our lives? Will they be able to say that the world is a happier, better place because of an idea which we had and started? Does it matter if they do not trace the start of it back to us? Isn't it more important that the good idea should prosper rather than that the person who started it should get all the praise?

A Prayer:

Lord Jesus, help to understand that the small things in life matter; may we not give up if no-one seems interested at first in a new idea, especially if it is a good idea which will help others and improve some part of the world. May we know that the really important things are having a kind and loving heart, living good lives and speaking good words - even in the smallest and seemingly unimportant parts of life. So may we all help to make the world a better and happier place.

Hymns: - The Church Of God A Kingdom Is
Jesus Shall Reign
These Things Shall Be; A Loftier Race
Help Us To Help Each Other Lord
God Of Concrete, God Of Steel

FRIENDLY HANDS

Have a large drawing of a hand on display; if possible also a drawing of a skeleton hand. Ask children for suggestions of things which they can do with their hands, and divide the suggestions into good and bad uses, *(friendly and unfriendly action)*. Some of the suggestions could be demonstrated, by leader or children, e.g. waving, punching, grabbing, stroking, helping, holding, etc.

What a lot of things you can do with your hands! How wonderfully made they are! All the little bones in them *(27 in each hand)* can move easily and simply without you even thinking about it. Yet a robot needs a great deal of complicated machinery to be put into operation before it can be set working, before it can do something as simple as picking up a pencil. God has made us much more wonderfully than that.

Have you ever looked carefully at a baby's hands? They are beautifully and perfectly formed, with tiny finger nails and tiny knuckles so that the fingers can bend. The baby can grasp your finger from its very early days. But it cannot do all the things that we can do until it gets older. It has to learn how to hold a knife and fork, tie a shoelace, play the piano, and so on; but all these things can be learnt and hands can do them easily once one knows how.

Ask for a few volunteers to demonstrate <u>caring hands</u> *(e.g. parent, nurse, gardener, pet owner, etc:)* <u>working hands</u> *(bus driver, shopkeeper, postman, road-mender, milkman, etc.)* If there is time, the children may like to guess the actions from the mimes, and then say if the use is right or wrong.

<u>How did Jesus use His hands?</u> *(For blessing children, healing blind, lame, deaf, etc., washing the disciples' feet, breaking bread, praying, once saving Peter from sinking in the water and drowning - all very good and friendly uses).*

Our hands will do as our brains tell them. Therefore it is important that we use brains in the right way. We have a choice, for God gave us free will to choose between good and bad. He showed us through Jesus the good ways, and if we follow that way of using our hands, we shall do well; but if we choose the bad and unfriendly ways, then we must not be surprised if we get into trouble. We must be ready for the consequences.

Our hands can be a marvellous power for good when working as God wants them to work; but they can also be a terribly bad thing when used to do things like pulling a trigger on a gun, wielding a knife to harm someone, stealing something that does not belong to you.

Someone once carved a statue of Christ. It was a beautiful statue, but it had no hands. The sculptor had done this deliberately to show that we were intended to be the hands of Christ. We were to use our hands for good in this world. Then we would be doing Christ's work on earth, which is what Christians are meant to do.

Can you think of some ways in which you can be Christ's hands today? - e.g. some ways in which you can use your hands for good - and stop them doing wrong things - and then act accordingly.

A Prayer:

Dear Father God, we praise You for our hands and all the many and wonderful things which they can do. Help us to use them in good and friendly ways so that they do not hurt or harm others. Help us too to remember that they are gifts from You, to do the work of Christ on this earth, so that we may remember to use them rightly in all we do. Thank You God for our hands.

Prayer of St. Theresa

*Christ has no body now on earth but yours,
No hands but yours, no feet but yours...
Yours are the feet with which He is to go about doing good,
And yours are the hands with which He is to bless us now.*

Hymn: -   Jesus' Hands Were Kind Hands.

RICHES

There was once a very rich lady who lived in a large and beautiful house. She had lots of lovely furniture and china and jewellery and clothes, and she had piles of money as well. She thought all these riches would make her very happy. 'I'm the wealthiest lady in the land,' she thought, 'no-one has so much as I have.' The strange thing was that, deep down inside her, she did not feel happy at all; in fact, she often felt very miserable.

The trouble was that she had no friends. She never dared to invite anyone in her house in case they stole some of her treasures while she was not looking; and she never dared to go out in case thieves broke in while she was away. So she spent much of her time on her own.

At last, one day, when she was feeling very low and miserable, she decided she would take a little walk in the country. She hadn't been out for years, and she thought she would like to see the fields and woods again. She was only away for about an hour, but while she was gone, a band of robbers broke into her house and took away everything they could carry. They even brought a big furniture van to carry the goods away. When the lady got back she realised that she had spent her life getting rich for nothing. Now she had nothing left.

A kind neighbour heard about this and took pity on her. 'Come and have tea with my family,' she said. 'We aren't rich, but you would be very welcome to what we have.'

Wearily, the lady agreed. She had nothing to stay in for now, and she thought she might as well see what a poor home looked like. She was very surprised to find that the family was very friendly. The father showed her his garden, where he was growing flowers and food for his family; he even gave her a bunch of flowers to take back with her. The lady was delighted; no-one had ever given her anything before; she had always bought everything, so that she could say 'that's <u>mine</u>.' The man's wife gave her a splendid home-made tea - a bit rough and ready perhaps, but it certainly tasted good. The children showed her their toys and invited her to play games with them. She even found herself crawling on the floor with the baby! Never before had she done anything so undignified - but she found it was fun.

When she went back home, she felt very different. For the first time in her life, she felt really happy. 'Money can't be all that important,' she thought. 'It isn't everything in life. I didn't know you could be rich in heart, as well. That seems to me to be far better, for no-one can steal a loving heart.'

She thought hard about it before she went to sleep, and she decided she would only collect the really important things in life in future, and she wouldn't care if she was poor.

For Older Children

What do you think are the really important things in your life? Usually they are the things which we think most about. What could you really not live without? Is it better to be short of money or short of friends? Money in itself is not wrong. It is the <u>love</u> of money, when we put it first in our lives, that is wrong.

Many people who have money use it wisely and unselfishly to help others, and there is nothing wrong in that. The wrong comes when it is used selfishly and wastefully. The people who think that getting rich is the most important thing in life will sooner or later learn their mistake. Jesus told a story once about a rich man who built bigger and bigger barns in which to store his grain and his goods; but when he died, all his goods went to other people, for he could not take his riches with him. <u>Read</u> Luke 12. 16-21.

A Prayer:

Lord Jesus, help us to see that it is not the things we <u>own</u> which matter so much as the things we <u>are</u> and <u>say</u> and <u>do</u>. Help us to be honest, kind, friendly and true, and to have loving hearts, for no-one can take these things away from us.

<u>Hymns:</u> -   Fill Thou My Life, O Lord My God
        The Wise May Bring Their Learning
        Here We Come With Gladness

'IN THE BEGINNING, GOD....'

Begin by reading aloud Genesis ch. 1 vv 1-29. Ask the children to listen carefully and to note things which God made. The piece may be read in sections, so that the children do not have to remember too long a list - e.g. Verses 1 - 8 *(light, dark, day, night, waters, sky, heaven)*; verses 9 - 19 *(earth, sea, plants, trees, sun, moon, stars)*; verses 20 - 29 *(birds, fish, animals, people)*. *(NB: check the words used in the version of the Bible from which you will be reading; they may differ slightly)*. Most versions of the Bible begins with the words, 'In the beginning, God....' *(or similar wording)*. God was there before there was anything. He always has been and always will be there. Ask child wearing something woollen to come out; ask where wool comes from *(sheep)*; who made the sheep? *(God)*. Similarly cotton *(cotton plants, made by God)*; the table *(made from wood, from trees, from God)*; something steel *(from metal, from ore in hillsides, put there by God)*; house *(from bricks, made from clay, put in earth by God)*, etc. *(Ask children to repeat, 'In the beginning, God...')*

<u>Story</u>: One day some boys were playing being spacemen in the garden. They were dressed in strange-looking clothes, helmets, and so on, and were making such a noise that father came out to see what it was all about.

'We're so high up,' said Simon, 'that we can see the world just like God can - sort of millions of miles away.'

'I don't quite agree with that,' said father; 'for God isn't <u>just</u> millions of miles away from us. He is also right here with us all the time - even though we cannot see Him. While men are trying to go higher and higher upwards, with God the movement is the other way. He came down to earth in the shape of Jesus Christ. He came to show us what God is like, and to live in us and with us for ever, even though we can't see Him. He wants us to live lives like Jesus in the world.'

'So isn't being an astronaut a good thing?' asked one of the boys, pausing for breath as he brought his rocket to a standstill.

'A very good thing,' answered Simon's father. 'I'm sure God wants us to find out about all the wonderful things He has created. After all, He is King of the world and King of space too. There would be just nothing if it wasn't for God. Yet He knows all about every one of us, even down to the smallest sparrow.'

'Coo!' said Simon. 'He must be quite the most important person that ever there was!'

'That's right,' said father. 'He is.'

For Older Children

Whatever we think about the details of the creation, whether we believe it was made in six days or whether we believe it evolved slowly, it is still God's world. It could not have been conceived by any human brain; it is essential that there must be an outside Power *(God)* controlling and overseeing all. Human beings can do many great things, and are learning all the time to do more and more, but the one thing they can never do is to create life. The cleverest man in the world cannot so much as make one single, living blade of grass.

A Prayer:

Thank You God for the countless wonderful things which You have made; for earth, air and sky, for the sea, rolling waves and running rivers; for earth and all growing things - trees with strong trunks and myriad leaves, plants and flowers with strong scents and lovely colours; for cuddly, furry animals and beautiful birds; for people, families and friends, and for all the fun and friendship we can have together.

(Silent pause to allow children to add any things for which they particularly want to praise God).

We praise You God that You made it all and that You have the whole world in Your hands. Thank You, our wonderful God.

Hymns: - He's Got The Whole World In His Hands
(It is suggested that children might like to clap to the rhythm; and then to add verses of their own. *(e.g. 'He's got flowers and trees in His hands'. 'He's got all the children in His hands', and so on).*
All Creatures Of Our God And King.

GOOD NEWS (THE BIBLE)

(This Assembly requires two children to be prepared to come in as newsboys or girls, and to say a very short speech, preferably already learnt, but if not then it may be read. The children should be rehearsed beforehand so that they call out their parts loudly and realistically).

<u>1st child</u>: *(entering with sack of newspapers if possible)* 'News! News! Terrible murders! Disaster in Africa! Thieves rob a bank! Family burnt in fire!.....

<u>Leader</u>: *(interrupting)* But that is all such <u>bad</u> news. Haven't you anything to read which is <u>good</u> news?' *(news-seller looks puzzled).*

<u>2nd child</u>: *(entering holding up a Bible)* Here you are. I've got some good news! It's all in here *(holds up Bible and points to it)*. In fact, in this Bible there is the best news that ever there was!'

<u>Leader</u>: 'May I look?' *(takes Bible and turns over the pages slowly)* Yes, this is all about God, how He made the world and everything and all the people in it. There are stories of some of the people who loved Him and did as He said - people like Abraham, Moses, David and Joseph - and sometimes there are stories about people who didn't love Him. *(Hold up Bible to show how much is the Old Testament - about two-thirds of the book).* The Old Testament is the time before Jesus came to earth *(Then hold up the New Testament, from St. Matthew to end).* There are all sorts of other stories too in the New Testament - and the best news of all is here. It tells us about Jesus and how God sent Him into the world to save us. Listen to this! *(Read John 3.16 'For God so loved the world...' etc).* This really is the most wise and hopeful book I have ever seen. It is God's book.

Ask how many children have their own Bible at home. How many read it? Where do they keep it? It is not intended to stand a plant on, but to be <u>read</u>. It is meant to be a guidebook through life. If we get lost on the roads, we consult a map. If we get lost in life, not knowing what to do next perhaps, then the Bible shows us the sort of life we should be living. But it is no good if you don't read it and so get to know it. You cannot wait until you are in trouble and then expect the Bible to produce the answer for you like magic. When the Queen is given a Bible at her Coronation, the Archbishop says, '... we present you with this Book, the most valuable thing this world affords.' Note that: it is <u>the most valuable</u> thing in the world - not in terms of money, but in its value in helping us to live as God wants us to live.

<u>For Older Children</u>

There are lots of different sorts *(versions)* of the Bible, not only in English but in thousands of languages all over the world too. It is constantly being up-dated and translated as different tongues and dialects are found which do not have the Bible in their own language.

There are several different versions in English *(the Authorised version, the Revised Version, the Revised Standard Version, the New English Bible, the Good News Bible, the New International Version, etc)*.
(Demonstrate to the children as many different versions as possible, and if there is time, let them come and look at them more closely). The Bible is not just one book; it is 66 different books, all bound together in one volume - 39 in the Old Testament and 27 in the New Testament. The Old Testament contains books of History, Law, Drama, Poetry and Prophecy; while the New Testament contains the four Gospels *(Life of Christ)* and the History of the Early Church *(Acts)*, 21 Letters *(Epistles)*, and a book of prophecy *(Revelation)*.

Children may like to show their own Bibles, if they have them with them, and, if illustrated, may like to show their favourite pictures. The whole point of the exercise is to get them to appreciate and value the Bible. Children of other faiths may be invited to show their holy books too.

A Prayer:

Lord God, we thank You for the Bible, a truly wonderful book. Help us to read it, treasure it and understand it, so that we may find out more about You and Your plans for us in this world. May its words be our guide through life, so that we may show forth Your love both in words and deeds.

Hymns: - The Best Book To Read Is The Bible

Read Your Bible, Pray Every Day
(Point out that to 'grow' here does not mean to grow in stature, but to grow as a better person, more like God every day).

KEEPING YOUR TEMPER
(for very young children)

One day, when it was very hot and sultry, a cat, a duck and a robin were sunning themselves on the farm. The cat was stretched out on a grassy bank, the duck was swimming on the edge of the nearby pond, and the robin was looking down from an overhanging branch of the tree; he didn't quite trust the cat, although he seemed friendly enough. So busy were they all, discussing the oddities of other creatures on the farmyard, that they did not notice a big black cloud coming nearer and nearer. Suddenly there was a violent clap of thunder and the rain came down in torrents.

The field was a long way from any real shelter, and the cat was furious. He hated getting his sleek fur wet, and he loathed it when something unexpected happened. 'Why couldn't we have had some warning?' he grumbled, as he set off for the shelter of the barn, as fast as he could.

'It doesn't worry me,' said the duck, swimming happily. 'The water just runs off my back and does not upset me in the slightest.'

'It's not quite the same for me,' chirped the robin, who was trying to shelter under a large leaf. 'I must admit I don't care much about the rain, but no doubt it is making quite a few puddles in the path; so when it stops, I shall hop over to one of them and have a bath. You have to make the best of things, you know.'

On the way to the barn, the cat met the sheepdog, with whom he was usually quite friendly.

'Good day,' said the sheepdog politely. 'Quite a sudden storm.'

'Grrrr', snarled the cat, which made the sheepdog wonder what he had said which had offended the cat.

Before he went to sleep that evening, the robin flew to the old oak tree to tell the wise old owl about the storm. The owl said, 'I would have thought that cat would have had more sense. I know it isn't very nice getting one's fur wet, but that's really no reason to get bad-tempered. The sheepdog told me he was quite hurt by the cat's rude behaviour.'

'The duck didn't let the storm worry him,' said the robin.

'No, and I wish more people were like him,' replied the owl. 'So many people get worked-up and bad-tempered when things go wrong, and they just upset everybody else around them.'

'Well I didn't feel too happy myself, I admit,' said the robin.

'No, but at least you had the sense to make the best of it,' said the owl.

When things go wrong and you get cross about it, you almost always make things worse. If you lose your temper and say rude and unkind things to those around you, then you make them feel bad too. If they cannot control their tempers, they will probably start saying unkind things back to you. That is how quarrels (and sometimes wars) start. If, when we get ruffled, we could ask for Jesus's help, and then remember not to vent our rage on other people, then the trouble would soon be over. Jesus said, 'Blessed are the peacemakers, for they shall be called the sons of God.' *(Matt. 5.9)*. We all feel that we want to shout and rage when things go wrong, but we have to learn to check these feelings, and to try and say something helpful and kind instead. This is not an easy lesson to learn. We have to let the wrong things run off us like the water on the duck's back; we do not have to be disagreeable as the cat was to the sheepdog. The robin in the story was perhaps the most sensible, as he resolved to make the best of the situation.

A Prayer:

O Lord God, help us to check our tempers when things go wrong in life. Show us that to be truly great, we must learn not to reply angrily, but to forgive and to make the best of the things which happen to us. So shall we learn to be better followers of your way.

Hymns: - Blest are the pure in heart.
              O Jesus, I have promised....

MUSIC

(Have some music played, either on piano or tape recorder, as the children come in to Assembly. Preferably quiet, worshipful music which will induce a mood of reverence. Also pin up pictures of musical instruments and people making music round the room. It may also be possible to have a display of musical instruments - e.g. violins, recorders, etc. all grouped round the piano).

What music have you heard already today? *(Radio, TV, birds singing, someone whistling in street, church bells?)* Which of you plays any instrument? *(Ask for show of hands for recorder, piano, violin, etc).* Who likes singing?

There is all sorts of music in the world, and it would be a very dull place if there weren't. The church bells call us to worship in this country - have you ever listened carefully to hear exactly how many bells are ringing at a church which you know? But if you were in some parts of Africa, for instance, you might be called to church by a drumbeat.

Music can put us in many moods. Sometimes it makes us feel happy and jolly and ready to dance, other times it makes us feel quiet, sometimes it makes us feel sad. Did you notice the music which was being played as you came to Assembly today? How did that make you feel?

In the Bible we read how we can praise God on various instruments, and with singing and dancing. King David, who was once a shepherd, played his harp, especially before King Saul to cheer him when he was feeling unhappy. We also read that David danced before the Lord to honour Him *(2 Sam. 6.14).*

In the Psalms, many of which were written by David, we read of many musical instruments being played to praise God. One such Psalm is the last one in the Psalter *(N°. 150)*, and as it is read, listen to find out how many instruments are mentioned.

<u>Read</u> Psalm 150. *(It mentions seven instruments, and dancing, as ways of praising God).*

Did you notice the first three words and the last three? *(Praise the Lord!)*

For Older Children

What part do you think music should play in our worship? Is it always important to have hymns? *(If we do, they need to be carefully chosen, for people learn a great deal of their theology through hymns, which they often remember much longer than they remember spoken words. Therefore it is vital to check that the hymns do not contain any misleading theology).*

Is a church service or an Assembly as realistic if it does not include some singing?

Is it essential to have a choir in a church? Members practice, usually weekly, so that they can get the music as perfect as possible in order to be able to lead the worship of God. The good choir also leads the spoken parts, and is there so that God's worship can be the very best that we can offer. If we were going to Buckingham Palace to see the Queen, we should take great care in preparing all that we were to say or do. Should we not therefore prepare equally thoroughly when we go to worship God who is the King of Kings?

A Prayer:

Thank You God for the gift of music - for the people who write the tunes, for those who make the instruments and for those who play them. Thank You for our voices, which we can also use in Your praise. May our worship be as beautiful and as perfect as we can make it, and may our lives as well as our worship be always pleasing in Your sight.

Hymns:

- Let All the World In Every Corner Sing
  (Draw attention to the title of your hymn book if it contains such words as 'sing' or 'praise').
  Praise The Lord! Ye Heavens Adore Him.
  Give Me Joy In My Heart, Keep Me Praising.

FOR THE GLORY OF GOD

(If the assembly takes place in a church, try and have it facing a stained glass window, if there is one. If in a hall, have a picture of a stained glass window, also pictures of church buildings, details of carvings, etc).

Who has seen a window with coloured glass in it? Why was it put there? Surely glass like that keeps out a lot of the light?

In the days before most people could read, this sort of glass, called stained glass, was often put in church windows to help people to understand the Bible and the things of God better. Such windows were the church's picture book. There would be scenes from Bible stories, pictures of Bible people and other saints, all of which helped those in church to know more about God. The glass also helped the church to look more beautiful, and because nothing but the best is ever good enough for God, people wanted to make His house, the church, look as lovely as possible.

If you look carefully at some of these windows, you may find the words, 'To the Glory of God....' written in them. This was because the makers did their beautiful work chiefly to honour God - to His glory, as we say.

This was true of a lot of other work which went into such buildings. The men did the very best work they could; even a little bit of carving, high up on a pillar, where no-one was likely to see it, was made as perfectly as possible. God could see it, and it was all done for His glory.

There has been stained glass in this country for about 1300 years, though most of the glass we see is not nearly as old as that. Coloured glass was made by adding metallic oxides to the glass as it was melted; cobalt coloured it blue, iron made it red, copper made it green, and so on. A thin layer of this coloured glass was put over the white glass, and it was then cut into shapes. Smaller details, like faces and drapery, were painted on. The panes were then baked and re-laid on the table, to be fastened together with grooved strips of lead. So the picture was formed. These strips made a strong black outline to the design. Then the panel was put into an iron frame, which often had patterns in it too, and these patterns were used as part of the design.

What is your aim when you do things, when you make things? Is it just to please yourself? Or to please someone else? Or is it, like the stained glass makers, for the glory of God?

If we do anything for the glory of God, it must obviously be the very best work we can do - for nothing but the best is good enough for God. We shall find that it is much more enjoyable to strive for excellence in any work - even a page of homework - rather than to be content with any old slipshod work which pleases nobody, not even yourself.

St. Paul, when he was writing a letter to the Colossians, told them about this. He said, 'Whatever you do, work at it with all your heart, as working for the Lord, not for men....' *(Col. 3.23 - NIV)*.

A Prayer:

We praise You, O God, for all the beautiful things which have been made, especially for beautiful buildings, beautiful glass, intricate carvings, paintings and delicate embroidery. These things were done for Your glory by craftsmen who were skilled in those arts and who used their skills in the best way they knew.
May everything we do be as good as we can make it, so that we may feel that our work is for Your glory too.

Hymns: - The Wise May Bring Their Learning
To God Be The Glory
Come and Praise The Lord Our King

Section B: Mainly for Juniors

DETERMINATION
(Mary Jones and Her Bible)

If you want to achieve anything very much, do you stick at it no matter what the difficulties may be - or do you give up when the going gets tough?

Mary Jones was a very poor Welsh girl, who could not go to school as there wasn't one near enough. When her father had finished his work as a weaver for the day, he would tell Mary a story. Sometimes they were true stories from the Bible, but always he <u>told</u> them from memory, because there was no Bible in the house. How Mary wished for a Bible of her own!

One day her father had some good news. A little school was to be opened two miles away across the hills. Mary was delighted, and though only ten, she cheerfully walked the two miles each way to school every day. Before long she had learnt to read. Farmer Evans, who lived nearby, had a Bible and he let Mary come and read it; but this was not the same as having her own Bible. So she began to save up every penny she could by helping other people with their work. She wasn't paid very much, and it took six years before she had saved enough money for a Bible.

Then one day she heard that a Mr Charles in Bala had some Bibles for sale. But Bala was twenty-five miles away! Undaunted, Mary set off early one morning to walk the twenty-five miles. She went barefoot, carrying her only pair of shoes, so that they wouldn't be too worn out to put on when she got there. It was a very long, tiring walk, but at last, Mary reached the home of Mr Charles.

'I'm afraid I have only three Bibles left,' said Mr Charles sadly, 'and they are all promised for other people.'

Mary was so disappointed at this that she broke down and cried. Mr Charles saw how very much she wanted a Bible, and so he managed to persuade one of the people to whom he had promised a Bible to wait a little longer, and he gave that Bible to Mary.

Happily, Mary gave him the money she had saved, and set off cheerfully homewards with her Bible in her hand.

Meanwhile, Mr Charles saw what a great need there was for Bibles - not only in Welsh, but in other languages too. So he went to London to plead for more Bibles for people like Mary, who were longing for Bibles and could not get them. He had started something bigger than he knew. For that request led to a meeting which founded a special Society to provide Bibles for people all over the world in their own languages. That Society, the Bible Society, is still working today, nearly 200 years after Mr Charles had started it by his request.

In this country, we can easily buy a Bible in our own language if we wish, but there are thousands of people in the world who cannot yet do so.

The Bible Society today is a very busy organisation. Its headquarters are at Stonehill Green, Westlea, Swindon, and it produces Bibles in many languages. Millions of people in the world cannot afford to buy a Bible of their own, so the Bible Society has a club (called *Bible-A-Month Club*) where people agree to give a certain amount of money each month so that someone in another land can have a Bible. They also produce special children's Bibles in all sorts of languages. It is hoped that, by the year 2,000, 69.3 million children able to read could have or will be able to see a copy of the printed Scriptures. That will still leave countless numbers without a Bible or unable to see one. They are thrilled when they get their own Bible, and often it becomes their most treasured possession.

Meanwhile the work of translating into new languages and making more Bibles continues daily.

Prayer

We thank You, God, for the Bible, that wonderful book which tells about You and Your Son, Jesus Christ. Thank You that we can have it in our language and can buy copies so easily. Help the work of the Bible Society so that people all over the world may be able to own a Bible and read the good news for themselves.

Hymns: - The Bible Tells Of God's Great Plan
God Has Given Us A Book Full Of Stories

BRAVERY
(Bishop John Coleridge Patteson)

Sometimes we think that only evil people are likely to be murdered, but today's story is of a good, brave man, who was murdered on a South Sea Island. The island was Nukapu, and the man was John Coleridge Patteson. He was a bishop, which means he was a leader of the Church.

When he grew up, he became very impressed by a man named George Augustus Selwyn, who himself was later made Bishop of New Zealand. John Patteson decided to become a clergyman, and when he had done so, Mr Selwyn suggested that he went out to the South Seas to start missionary work there.

The work which Patteson started later became known as the Melanesian Mission. Melanesia consists of a lot of small islands north-east of Australia, with a lot of sea between them. *(show map)* So, to do his work, Patteson had to use a ship to get around. His ship was called 'The Southern Cross.' Not only had he to learn a lot about the sea and about sailing, but he also had to learn the languages the people spoke, so that he could talk to them.

He went around telling people about the love of God, and he also started a college for boys. After a time, he was made a Bishop, when he was only 34. He was very successful in educational work, and did much to help the islanders in all sorts of other ways. He had a great love for the people and many came to love him too.

One day, he landed alone on the island of Nukapu. He wasn't afraid, for he had been teaching the love of God for some ten years. Suddenly, without warning, a group of islanders sprang out and killed him. Some of their own men had been kidnapped earlier, and the islanders committed this murder out of revenge - which is always quite wrong and invariably leads to more trouble. The natives then put Bishop Patteson's body on a canoe and floated it out to sea.

When the people in Britain heard about it, they were very sad and a special Day of Prayer was held. Queen Victoria, who was on the throne at the time, was very upset. The nation mourned the loss of a great man.

But the work of the Melanesian Mission did not stop. Other people carried it on - telling people about God, helping to heal the sick, and teaching them to love and serve the Lord. The work still goes on today. There are more schools and hospitals, and many islanders have been baptised. So Bishop Patteson's work continues.

It takes some bravery to go to a foreign country and to teach the people about God's love. One of the great beliefs of Christianity is that all men are equal in God's sight, no matter what race or colour they may be. Quarrels often break out between people of different races, often just because they are different; but this would not be so if we all followed Jesus' teaching to love our neighbours *(i.e. everyone we meet)*. In the story which Jesus told about the Good Samaritan *(Luke 10. 25-37)*, it was a Samaritan *(a man of a different race from the wounded Jew)* who came and bound up his wounds and took pity on him. The Samaritan did not say, 'It's only a Jew, I won't bother to help him.' He gave him all the care and love he could. Likewise Bishop Patteson gave all the care and love he could to the people among whom he worked. That is really what loving our neighbour means.

A Prayer:

O Father God, help us to be caring and understanding towards other people, especially those who come from a different country or who live a different sort of life from ours. May we see that we cannot truly love You unless we also love our neighbours, for we know that You love all people and that you want us to love them too.

Hymns: - Lord Of The Loving Heart
In Our Work And In Our Play
Go Forth And Tell
I Will Make You Fishers Of Men

HELPING BLINDNESS THROUGH BLINDNESS
(Father Jackson of Burma)

William Jackson lost his sight when he was only two years old. His mother would not let people pity him, and she insisted that he be treated exactly like his brothers and sisters and join in everything. So he climbed trees, rode a bike round the garden, slid down the cottage roof, and got into all kinds of mischief. His sensitive fingers were very clever with anything mechanical, and he enjoyed such jobs as repairing clocks, and mending any machinery.

He went to a special school for the blind, and there he learnt Braille and also music. It was not until he was confirmed that he decided he would be a clergyman. Being blind did not put him off. So he studied and was ordained and first worked in two places in the south of England.

Then he heard that there were many blind people in Burma and that nothing was being done to help them; he decided that he would go there himself. He learnt Burmese, and then went out to Burma to take charge of a school for blind boys, which needed someone to run it. Once there he shared fully in the life of the boys; he ate with them, dressed like them, swept floors and washed clothes - and the boys loved him. They called him APAY-GYI *(Big Father)*. There was no Braille reading system for them, so Father Jackson invented one. He hammered out the Braille on old kerosene tins, and rolled off copies using an old mangle. It was so good that soon the blind boys could read faster than the sighted boys.

There were many boys in the country who could not see and who did not come to school. So Father Jackson went out looking for them. He preferred to go to their homes and to talk to their parents first, so that the parents knew to whom they were entrusting their child. These long walks often meant journeys into the jungle and the possibility of stepping on snakes or meeting thieves. But Father Jackson was unafraid, putting his trust in God.

His school grew so much that soon a new one was needed, and Father Jackson decided to design it himself. He put in it several new inventions to help the blind to find their way about, such as guide rails in the corridors, and slightly raised marks on the floor to warn the boys of a corner or a doorway.

In the school the boys learnt handicrafts, making toys, baskets, mats and chairs and repairing boots and tuning pianos. Their goods sold so well that soon the school was self-supporting. When the boys left school, they were able to take jobs, and soon realised that to be blind did not mean they were useless. Always Father Jackson taught them of God's love for them. He produced plays which helped to teach Christian truths. Through him the boys grew to love the Christ whom he served, and that was all the reward he wanted.

Father Jackson was an amazing man who triumphed over a severe handicap. He had to cope with a new country, a new language, a new climate, new manners and customs, all without the benefit of sight. His spirit refused to be defeated, no matter how hard the task seemed. Many of us, who can see, would not do nearly so much; the temptation to give up would be very strong. But Christians know that however difficult life seems and however insuperable the problems appear, Jesus is there to give strengthening help when it is needed. All we have to do is to ask Him and to trust Him implicitly, and the help will come. This is the way a true Christian faces life.

<u>A Prayer:</u>
Lord Jesus, thank You for the work of Father Jackson and the great influence he had over the blind children in Burma. Help and bless all blind people and show us what we can do to help those who cannot see. Thank You for our own eyes and for the wonderful world which we can see with them.
(Short silence, to think of any special things you have seen lately for which you wish to say thank you).

<u>Hymns</u>: - I Sing A Song Of The Saints Of God.
             Teach Me, My God And King.

AIMING HIGH - (Henry Martyn)

"Expect great things from God; attempt great things for God." This was the motto of Henry Martyn, a brilliant Cambridge scholar who went to India in 1806 as chaplain of the East India Company.

When he arrived in Calcutta, he was delighted to meet William Carey, a great Baptist missionary, and together the two men plunged into a talk about the work before them. Carey was full of ideas, one of which was a suggestion for an annual meeting of missionaries from all over the world. It was not until 1910 that the World Missionary Conference met in Edinburgh.

Carey and Martyn decided that there were such multitudes of people in India that no man could preach to more than a fraction of them. The best way was to translate the Bible into their own languages. There were many different languages in India, and Martyn began, in the spare moments in his chaplaincy work, to translate the New Testament into Hindustani. He mastered the language quickly and made an excellent translation which was a model for many years. He next turned his hand to translations into Arabic and Persian. The Persian translation proved very difficult, and he decided that the only way to get it perfect was to go to Persia.

His friends were appalled. 'Impossible!' they said. 'You can't! Do you know what the weather is like there at this time of year? It's so hot that it bursts the thermometer!'

But nothing stopped Martyn when he had made up his mind. *'Attempt great things for God'* was still his motto, and off he set for Persia.

The heat was almost unbearable, but Martyn worked as best he could in it and had some help from Persian friends. So hard did he work that he had translated the New Testament into Persian in nine months. The Persian scholars were most impressed.

Martyn's health was suffering and he was now a sick man. He knew he must go home. It was on the way back that, weak with fever, he died at Tokat in Asia Minor. He had lived and died for the Kingdom of God.

On coming to India he had felt that he must do something

for God. He had indeed lived for this purpose and in the end he 'burnt out' for God. Henry Martyn aimed high. He knew that God can do great things and that we can do great things also, if we work with Him. This was the meaning behind his motto 'Expect Great Things From God; Attempt Great Things For God'. Often we are content to do less than our best; we are content to take the easy way out and to give up if there seem to be too many problems and difficulties in the way. This way of life may seem easier, but it is not nearly so satisfying as striving for excellence and overcoming the problems we meet.

Someone once said, talking of buildings, that a difficult site is the architect's opportunity. In other words, the architect has a real chance to erect a fine building on land where there are problems. If he works to overcome those problems, then he really achieves something. On the other hand, if he looks at the problems, grumbles that they are too hard, and then goes away to find something simpler, then he has taken the easy way out and probably not achieved very much.

A wise old man, giving advice to his grandson, who was facing problems at school, said, 'Difficulties were made to be overcome.' It is the way we look at problems that matters and that helps to form our characters.

A Prayer:

We thank You, heavenly Father, for the Bible, and for all those who have overcome great problems in order to translate it into other languages, so that people in many different countries may read it for themselves. Thank You, particularly for Henry Martyn who worked himself to his death in the service of God. May we never run away from the hard things in life, but instead may we expect great things from God, and attempt great things for Him.

Hymns: - When The Road Is Rough And Steep
He Who Would Valiant Be
Stand Up, Stand Up For Jesus!

EACH ONE TEACH ONE (Frank Laubach)

Frank Laubach wanted to be a pioneer. He was born in Pennsylvania, and when he grew up he went out to the Philippine Islands. There he found some dark-skinned people called Moros, who were Muslims. The Americans had tried to start schools for them, but the Moros had not understood and had set fire to the buildings. Laubach wanted to tell them about God, but they were fearful and moved away when they saw him coming. He became very depressed and was ready to give the whole thing up. But one night he felt that God was telling him, *'You have failed because you did not love the people enough. You felt that you were better than they are.'*

Frank Laubach suddenly realised that no matter what colour a man's skin, God loves him just the same. Laubach felt he must tell this great truth to the Moros, and to be fair, he felt he must also learn about their religion. So he went humbly to a group of Muslim priests and asked them to teach him about their holy book, the Koran. It worked, and gradually the people became more friendly towards him. Teaching them was more difficult, because their language had never been written down. There wasn't even an alphabet. Laubach decided he would have to work one out, write it down, and then teach the people to read. One of the Moros and a Filipino missionary agreed to help him, and in six weeks they had written down about thirteen hundred words. It seemed that God was guiding their work.

They found a disused cinema which they were able to convert into a church, and a trader gave them a shop to use as a school. Then a friend sold them a heavy printing press very cheaply, but there seemed nowhere solid enough for it to stand - until they discovered that, under the rotting floor boards of the building they wanted to use for printing, there was a solid concrete base of exactly the size they needed!

Laubach and his friends began printing, but now the problem was teaching the Moros to read, and Laubach began by using charts with pictures.

The village chiefs came to learn to read first, for they were the leaders and the people would follow what they did. But to teach everyone was an enormous task and Laubach felt they would need hundreds of teachers - and there was no money to pay them even had they been available. Then one of the chiefs said, 'This campaign cannot stop for lack of money. Everyone who learns must also teach. <u>Each one teach one</u>.' It was a wonderfully simple idea! People could not have another reading lesson until they had first taught someone else the lesson they had just learned.

So the campaign forged ahead, and the number of people who could read grew every day. The Government wanted Laubach to give lessons all over the Philippines, and leaders from all over the world wanted him to come and teach their people to read. Far and wide he went, learning new languages, teaching more people to read. In this way he did a great deal to help world literacy - and he was a great pioneer, which was what he had wanted to be.

'Each one teach one' is an excellent motto. It points out that, if you have anything which is good, do not keep it to yourself, but share it; spread the good news around. This is how the Kingdom of God grew, from its earliest days in Jerusalem. It began with the disciples, twelve frightened men, who were empowered by the Holy Spirit on the Day of Pentecost, and who went out, no longer afraid, to fulfil Jesus's words, to go out into all the world and teach all nations.... (Matthew 28.19). That must have seemed an impossible task for only twelve men. But those they taught taught others, and so the Word of God has spread throughout the world. There are now millions of Christians. We must not let it stop there.

<u>A Prayer</u>:

Thank You Lord for all the books we have and that we can learn to read so easily. Thank You for story books, lesson books, and most of all for Your holy book, the Bible. May we remember to share the good news about You, and so help to bring about Your Kingdom on earth. In this way we shall be helping the good news of the Gospel to spread throughout the world.

<u>Hymns</u>: - Wide, Wide As The Ocean
　　　　　　 We Want To Tell You Of Jesus' Love
　　　　　　 Remember All The People

FIGHTING DISEASE (Father Damien)

Joseph de Veuster was a young Belgian who joined a religious society when he was 19. Here the men took new names, and Joseph's name was Damien. As part of his work, he was sent out to some islands in the Pacific Ocean. Later he was put in charge of parts of the islands of Hawaii and Molokai, where he worked among the people and built churches for them.

However, he was worried that many of the people had a horrible disease called leprosy. This meant that they were not allowed to mix with other people, since everybody was afraid of catching the disease from them. So people with leprosy had to keep right away from their families and friends, and from everyone else, and as a result they led lonely and unhappy lives mixing only with one another. There was a settlement of lepers at Molokai, where they had been sent and forgotten about; no-one was there to look after them, and so they died alone and in misery.

In 1873 Father Damien asked to go to Molokai himself, so that he could do something to help those suffering from leprosy. It was a brave thing to do, but Damien was determined to go where such great help was needed. There were about six hundred of them, and Damien set about building hospitals, schools and churches for them.

The lepers had been used to people running away from them, so they were very surprised when they found that Father Damien did not run away. He remembered how Jesus had behaved with lepers, how He had gone up to them, touched and healed them. So Father Damien went up to them too and did all he could to help them. It was no good telling them about the love of God if he did not show it himself.

So he told them about the love of Jesus, and for those who were well enough, he found some useful work to do. He knew that they would feel better if they were doing something to help.

One day, when Father Damien had been there for several years, he happened to drop some boiling water on his foot. He found that he felt no pain at all, and he realised that this meant he had caught leprosy himself.

For as long as he could, he continued to stay with and work among the lepers. In some ways, now that he was a leper himself, the work was easier, for he could talk about 'us' instead of 'you', and he felt the lepers knew he could really understand their difficulties.

He died at the age of 49, having given his life to fighting disease and to making easier the life of those who suffered.

Find out all you can about the disease of leprosy. Whereas once it could not be cured, nowadays, thanks to a lot of dedicated and wonderful work by doctors and others, it often can be cured if it is attended to in its early stages.

In Bible times, and for long afterwards, people were afraid to go anywhere near someone suffering from leprosy. So much so, that the lepers used to carry a little bell which they rang, shouting 'Unclean! unclean!' to warn everyone to keep away. Jesus had no such fears. He touched and cured them. Read one of the stories in the Bible about Him curing lepers - *(e.g. Luke 17. 11-19)*. Father Damien had no fear either, and the reason was that he was unselfish. He did not think how the disease would affect <u>him</u>; rather he thought of how he could help <u>them</u>. This is the true spirit of consideration, of putting other people before yourself.

<u>A Prayer:</u>
Thank You God for brave unselfish people who often leave home and travel far in order to help others. We ask You to bless them and to help them as they go out to teach and to show other people of Your love. Keep them safe in danger and give them strength and courage and the joy of knowing that they are working with You.
May we too learn the same spirit of unselfishness, so that we may leave the world a better place.

<u>Hymns:</u> - Remember All The People Who Live In Far-off Lands
From Thee All Skill And Science Flow
Be Valiant, Be Strong

TELLING THE TRUTH (Micaiah)

How easy do you find it to tell the truth, always? Isn't it often easier to tell a lie, to get out of a jam? Here is a story of a man who was determined to tell the truth at all costs.

One day King Jehoshaphat of Judah went to Ahab the King of Israel who asked, 'Will you help me get Ramoth-Gilead from the King of Syria? After all, it really belongs to us.'

'I'm ready when you are,' said Jehoshaphat agreeably, and so is my army. But let us ask God first.'

So Ahab called in all the prophets of the land; there were about 400 of them. 'Yes,' said the prophets. 'You go and attack Ramoth; God will see that you will win.'

But Jehoshaphat was still not too happy. He had a nasty feeling that the prophets were not telling the truth, and that they were only answering as they did to please the King.

'Isn't there any other prophet we could ask?' he said.

'There is one,' replied Ahab. 'He is named Micaiah, but I hate him. He never prophesies any good things; it's always something bad which he says will happen.'

But he sent for Micaiah all the same, and an official went to get him. The two kings, Ahab and Jehoshaphat, sat on their thrones dressed in their royal robes, and the four hundred prophets went on telling them what they thought they wanted to hear. Meanwhile the official who had gone to get Micaiah was telling him what the prophets had said. 'So you had better say the same,' he warned Micaiah.

Micaiah glared at him. 'I will say just what God tells me to,' he said.

When he arrived, Ahab asked him whether he and Jehoshaphat should attack Ramoth-Gilead or not.

Micaiah replied mockingly, 'Oh, attack, of course, and you'll win.'

Ahab could see that Micaiah was mocking him and was not serious. 'Tell me the <u>truth</u>,' he ordered.

So then Micaiah warned that the armies would be scattered, like sheep without a shepherd, if they went to battle with Ramoth-Gilead. He said that Ahab's prophets had been telling lies.

'There you are,' said Ahab to Jehoshaphat. 'I told you he always prophesies bad things.' And he had Micaiah arrested and put in prison to be fed on bread and water until Ahab should return in safety.

But Ahab did not return safely. As he and Jehoshaphat were fighting, against Ramoth-Gilead, one of the Syrian soldiers shot an arrow which struck Ahab. By the evening he was dead.

So Micaiah had proclaimed God's message truthfully and fearlessly, even though there were 400 other prophets against him.

(If you want to read the story of Micaiah in your Bible, you will find it in 1 Kings ch.22).

The words which we speak can be thought of as like the toothpaste which we squeeze from the tube. In no way can you get it back into the tube again, and in no way can words which have been spoken be unsaid. It used to be said by some people, 'My word is my bond', meaning that what they had said was the truth and that they would stick to it. If it was a promise of something, then that promise would be kept. A bond is a binding agreement. People ought to be able to feel that they can trust us and that what we say is the truth. A truthful person is far more trustworthy than one who tells you what he thinks you want to hear or who tells lies to make things easier for himself.

<u>A Prayer</u>:

Heavenly Father, sometimes it is easier to say wrong things or to tell lies, especially if it gets us out of trouble. Help us at these times to be brave and honest, and to speak up truthfully, no matter how many others may seem to be against us. Help us at all times only to speak words which are true and right, for we know that nothing can keep the truth from You, who know all things.

<u>Hymns</u>: - O Jesus, I Have Promised
Father, Lead Me Day By Day
A Man Once Came From Galilee

BEING SINCERE

Long ago, some monks decided to build a monastery on what had been a marshy piece of ground. They drained the marsh so that they could grow crops, and they built a beautiful chapel where they could go to praise God. They went out visiting the sick and the poor, and when travellers came by the monastery, they asked them in and offered them food and shelter.

They worked long and hard, but the job they found hardest of all was singing! Mostly they were old men and their voices were cracked, and many of them were not very musical at all. But the Abbot *(the Head of the Monastery)* said they must continue to do their best and to praise God in their Services day by day.

One day a young traveller came to the monastery. He was cold and weary, and the kindly monks immediately offered him hospitality and shelter. Gratefully he agreed to stay the night, and asked whether he could do anything for them.

When the monks asked him what he did, he replied that he was a singer. The monks were delighted to hear this. Perhaps the traveller would sing the service for them in the chapel that evening. Then, for once, the Service would be sung properly and beautifully, they thought.

'Of course I will,' said the traveller. 'In fact, I have won many prizes for my fine voice.'

So that evening, all the monks kept silent in the chapel while the traveller sang his way through the evening service in his beautiful voice. He was very proud of himself and kept thinking how beautifully he was singing and how much better his voice was than those of the old men.

That night the Abbot had a dream. He dreamt that an angel came to him and asked, 'Where was your song of praise this evening?'

'But we had the Service as usual,' replied the puzzled Abbot, 'only it was sung more beautifully than it had ever been sung before.'

The angel shook his head. 'No sound of praises reached the heavens,' he said. 'All we heard was someone thinking how good he was and what a lovely voice he had.'

Then the Abbot knew that the young man had not really meant the praises he had been singing. His thoughts had been only on himself and his singing had not been sincere.

It has been said that the word 'sincere' comes from the two Latin words, 'sine' meaning 'without' and 'cera' meaning 'wax'. The reason given is that when the Romans ordered statues to be made, they knew that sometimes the sculptors would cover up cracks in their workmanship with wax, which could not be detected until the wax melted. Therefore they asked that the work should be 'sine cera', 'without wax'. If cracks or flaws had been repaired and covered with wax, it would make the work seem perfect when it was not.

Thus we say that people who do not try to hide anything are 'sincere'. The dictionary defines sincere as 'Free from pretence or deceit, the same in reality as in seeming or profession, not assumed or put on, genuine, honest, frank....' *(Concise Oxford Dictionary)*.

A Prayer:
Heavenly Father, help us to be honest and sincere in all we say and do. Make us ready to speak up for what we know is true and right, and never to try and hide things nor to make pretence. Forgive us for the times when we have not been sincere, and help us to do better in the days to come.

Hymns: - Come And Serve The Master
Take My Life And Let It Be
Yesterday, Today, For Ever

WHAT GOES INSIDE

Are you fussy about your food? Some boys and girls just hate green vegetables, and cabbage in particular. Others can't bear eggs, or cheese. Most people seem to like crisps or fish and chips or ice cream! Yet we have to take some care about what we eat so that we get a balanced diet, with enough protein, carbohydrates, and so on, and enough calories to keep up our right weight and strength.

But it isn't only what goes into our stomachs that is important. It is just as necessary to watch what goes into our minds. If you read a bad book or watch a bad film, and then let your mind continue to dwell on it, then that is just as bad for you as eating the wrong sort of food. If you make a habit of thinking unkind, disagreeable thoughts, then it upsets the whole of you; and to let such thoughts stay in your mind is as bad as having poisonous germs inside you.

You may wonder how you can stop it. After all, you can't help seeing and hearing wrong things sometimes. What you can do is to stop your mind dwelling on such things, and replace the bad thoughts by good wholesome ones. You cannot have two things in exactly the same place. A rose and a weed cannot grow in exactly the same spot. The things you think about most determine the sort of person you will become. If you think unkind angry thoughts for most of the time, then you will become an unkind angry person. You will start saying unkind angry things almost without realising it. If you think a lot of quarrelsome thoughts, then you will become a quarrelsome person. But if you try to think cheerful happy thoughts, then that is the sort of likeable person you will be. Moreover, you will be helping to make the world a happier place by your disposition.

In a way, your mind is like a camera, for the things in it are a picture of the kind of person you are.

St Paul has some good advice about it. He says *(Phil. 4.8)*,

'Whatever is true, whatever is honourable, whatever is just, whatever is pure, whatever is lovely, whatever is gracious, if there is any excellence, if there is anything worthy of praise, think about these things.' *(RSV)*.

Many people today are easily led by wrong things which other people want them to take part in. They think that because 'everybody does it', it must therefore be right. But in order to grow spiritually, *(as a Christian)*, you must have certain principles. What are the things you would refuse to do or read or take part in, no matter who persuaded you that it would 'be all right'? Would it affect you if people laughed at you because you would not take part? If you are in doubt and you take a stand, then it is more than likely that you are in the right.

A Prayer:

Dear Lord, help us keep a watch on our minds and to be able to tell right from wrong. If we are uncertain, give us the courage to ask advice from someone older; we also ask Jesus for His strength that we may grow more like Him day by day, so that we do and say only those things which we know to be right.

Hymns: - Soldiers Of Christ, Arise
Blest Are The Pure In Heart
Lord Of All Hopefulness

THE THREE MONKEYS
(See, Hear and Speak no Evil)

Have you ever seen a little model of three monkeys - one with its hands over its eyes, one with its hands over its ears, and one with its hands over its mouth? The monkeys convey the message 'See no evil, hear no evil and speak no evil' - which is quite a good motto for a young Christian to have.

In the last assembly *(What goes inside - pages 47 - 48)* we talked a little about seeing and hearing no evil so that we should not pollute our minds. Today we concentrate on the third one - Speak No Evil.

In the 3rd chapter of the Epistle *(or letter)* of James in the Bible, James tells us how important it is to control our tongues and to watch the words we speak. The tongue is only a little member of our bodies, but it can do great things *(James 3 v 5)*. It only takes one match to set a whole forest ablaze, and it only takes one little wrong word to start a whole host of trouble. So we must always be careful what we say.

When a pebble is thrown into a pond, the ripples go on and on. They cannot be stopped. The same is true of our words. Once said, they are likely to be repeated by other people and to go on spreading. We cannot 'un-say' them.

So we need to be sure that what we say is true and accurate. A wise man once said that if you are not certain whether to say something or not, then you must apply three tests: *(i)* Is it true? *(ii)* Is it necessary? *(iii)* Is it kind? If you can say 'yes' to all three of these questions, then it is safe to say what you were going to say.

There was once a man who talked too much *(as many of us do!)* and he asked a friend how he could curb his bad habit. The friend suggested he took a bag of feathers with him one day, and every time he spoke, he should put one feather on the ground. The man did this and then came and asked his friend, 'What next?'

'Go out tomorrow and pick them all up,' advised the friend. Of course, the man couldn't, as they had all blown away he knew not where, but it helped him to remember that his words could spread much further than he imagined, and that therefore he must be careful what he said.

<u>Reading</u>: James 3 vv 1-12.

Do you think the world would be a better place if we all took more care of the things we said? If we only spoke about other people after we had made certain our words were true, necessary and kind, would that be likely to put a stop to many quarrels and wars?

Sometimes you might hear a person say *(usually when someone has died)*, 'He *(or she)* never spoke a wrong word about anyone.' How good it would be if that could be said about you!

Whenever you see a box of matches, try and remember how one match could start a huge fire, and say to yourself 'ONE WORD CAN DO GREAT GOOD OR GREAT HARM'. Then try and make sure that all your words are '<u>Safety</u>-matches.' Do you think it is ever right to repeat something bad about someone else? Would it be a better world if we never spread gossip?

<u>A Prayer</u>:

Lord God, help us to keep a watch over our tongues today. May we say only those things which are true, necessary and kind, so that evil words about other people will not spread. Help us not to be quick to answer back, nor to carry on a quarrel; and may we never be ashamed to let others know that we belong to You, and are ready to follow in Your ways.

<u>Hymns</u>: - Take My Life, And Let It Be.
(Draw attention to v. 3 'Take my voice....')
Be Thou My Guardian And My Guide
Blessed Is The Man, The Man Who Does Not Walk

GIVING

There was once a rich man who sent a cheque for several hundred pounds to his church. When the vicar came to thank him, the man said, 'Oh that's all right, vicar. I've got everything I want in life and that cheque is just the bit I had left.'

'Then I am sorry, but I do not think I can take it,' said the vicar.

'Why ever not?' asked the puzzled man.

'Because just giving to God what you have left is not the right spirit of giving, I fear. God does not just want our leftovers; He wants us to give sacrificially.'

'Even when it is hundreds of pounds?' asked the rich man.

'Yes, no matter what the amount,' replied the vicar.

The man went away and thought about this. Then he wrote another cheque, many times larger than the first. 'That is what I would have spent on my new car,' he told the vicar, 'so it really is a sacrifice for me to give that.'

How do you give money to help others? To charities? Do you spend all that you want to spend on yourself, and then give any odd coin that might be left to good?' We need to arrange our giving to God, to charities or good causes properly. We need to budget for it. Just as we may set aside a certain amount of money for sweets and so on, so we should set aside the amount of money we intend giving to other causes than ourselves. The Jews used to reckon to give one tenth of their money back to God for His work. That may be a high standard for you, but it is better to set a certain amount apart, even if smaller, say, each week, than to give haphazardly.

Churches have to have money to run their buildings and pay their staff; they do not get grants from the Government. They have to pay for heating, lighting, books and so on. But they also give money for objects outside of themselves. Many churches give to poorer churches in other countries, they give to famine relief, and to aid people suffering from disasters. In fact, the Church was on the job building hospitals and schools long before ever Governments took the work on. If it wasn't for the Church, there still would not be schools and hospitals in some places.

So we know that our money given to such causes is used for very good work.

Jesus once told a young man, who was very rich, that the way he should live, after he had kept the commandments *(which the young man said he had kept)* was to sell his possessions and give to the poor. When the young man heard this, he was very sad, for he had great possessions and did not want to give them up.

Read Matthew 19 vv 16-22.

Does the spirit in which you give matter? Do you think it matters if you give grudgingly, grumbling to yourself that you don't really want to give, but you suppose you had better? The Bible tells us how we ought to give, in 2 Cor. 9 v 7, where St Paul tells us that 'God loves a cheerful giver.'

Jesus noted once, when He was sitting near the temple treasury, that many rich people gave a lot of money, whereas a poor widow gave only two small coins, which was all she had to live on. *(Mark 12. 41-44)*. Which gift do you think was the better one?

A Prayer:

Help us, Lord Jesus, to be generous and cheerful in our giving, to remember that many causes need our help, and that we often have enough and more than enough on which to live. Help us to give and not to count the cost, and to give cheerfully.

Hymns: - When I Survey The Wondrous Cross
(Draw attention to last verse and especially last line)
Fill Thou My Life, O Lord My God
Here We Come With Gladness

HANDICAPS - SHOWING CONCERN

Prepare for this assembly by having a few children ready with supposed handicaps - an arm in a sling, a hand with fingers bandaged, a child blindfolded, one on crutches, one with ears stopped with cotton wool, etc.

Then suggest that these children try some normal actions - those with injured hands or arm could try using a knife and fork; the one on crutches could try walking; the blindfolded one be asked to walk to a specific point; and the deaf one be asked to reply to a question spoken quietly. The problems encountered will be obvious.

This is sometimes called being handicapped. Ask children if they know of anyone with such problems. What difficulties did it cause them? Sometimes the problem may be hidden and not show. Someone may be feeling lonely and too scared to ask if he may join in a game. Someone else may be feeling out of things because he is in some way different.

What do you do about it? Do you go on playing your own games and say to yourself, 'It has nothing to do with me'? But if you really care for other people and are trying to lead a Christian life, then it has something to do with you.

Listen to this story of how Jesus dealt with a man who was deaf and also could not talk properly. The reason why some deaf people can't talk is that they have never heard any sounds, if they have been deaf from birth, and so have nothing to copy. We learn to speak by listening to others; you probably began talking by saying words which you heard your mother or father say. *(Read Mark 7: vv 31-37)*

In this story Jesus showed a very thoughtful concern. He knew how hard it is for a deaf person, who may perhaps have a little hearing, to hear and understand what is going on if he is in a crowd of people. He cannot hear clearly if there is a lot of other noise going on around him. But Jesus knew that, and he took the man away from the crowd where it was quieter to heal him *(v.33)*. He made signs, touching the man's ears and tongue, because the man could not have heard what Jesus was saying; so He had to show him. He also showed, by looking up to heaven, that the healing was coming from God.

Do you know of any other stories where Jesus showed kindness and concern? *(When He healed the blind, the lame, the lepers, the paralysed, etc.).*

Who shows concern today? Doctors, nurses, police, ambulance men, rescue services, etc., and anyone who tries to help somebody else.

There are lots of ways in which we can show concern today. Perhaps you might offer to read to someone who doesn't see very well; help someone to carry shopping; ask someone who seems left out to join in your games; hold open a door for someone to walk through - especially if that person has a lot to carry.

These may all be only small ways, but they are important. They are part of leading a good, caring life, or, to put it in a Christian way, loving your neighbour, as well as loving God.

If you love your neighbour (and that means anyone you meet) then you will be concerned about him or her and want to do anything you can to help. It is easy just to <u>say</u> you are sorry for him or her - anyone can do that; the caring and concerned person will <u>do</u> something to help.

<u>A Prayer</u>:
Father God, thank you for our strong bodies, good thoughts and loving hearts. Help us to notice when other people need us and that there is something which we can do to help. Jesus showed care and concern to all He met when He was on earth. Help us to be caring people too, so that we may grow more like Him in all we say and do.

<u>Hymn</u>: - Lord Of The Loving Heart
God Is Love, His The Care

GROWING IN PRAYER

One day, a certain girl called Jill was saying her prayers. She began with the Lord's Prayer *('Our Father.....'),* and then she went on to say, 'God bless mum, God bless Dad and the rest of my family, and make me a good girl, Amen.'

It so happened that her aunt, who was on a visit, heard Jill say these prayers, and she was a little surprised.

'Aren't you getting rather big for that kind of prayer, Jill?' she asked. 'After all, you are nearly ten now.'

Jill was puzzled. 'But I thought they were good prayers,' she said.

'Certainly they are; the Lord's Prayer particularly,' Aunt said. 'I was meaning the others. You don't seem to have changed them since I came to see you last year.'

Jill didn't think that mattered, but, as her Aunt explained, it does. The rest of our life does not stand still. We move into higher forms at school, our hair and our nails grow and have to be cut, we grow ourselves needing larger clothes sizes, and we study more and more advanced books. So our bodies and minds both grow. What sometimes does not grow is our souls - the spiritual side of our lives.

One of the ways our souls *(spirits)* can grow is through prayer. By praying we get to know more about God. As we get to know and understand Him a little better, so our Christian life grows and we are able to be of more help to Him in the world. It is hard work to go on working for a God whom we know very little about.

It is best to try and have a regular time for prayer, morning or evening or both. Morning and evening are good times because they help us to remember that each day in our life is given to us by God; so if we think of Him at the beginning and/or ending of each day, we can say our main prayers to Him at those times. It is a good habit to get into.

But you don't only pray at set times or in set places, like in church or in Assembly. You can pray *(which means talking to God)* at any time and in any place - on a bus, in a train, walking along the road, just by remembering God and telling

Him what you are about to do, or asking for His help. But we need to grow in prayer, learning new ones and new things to talk to God about. If we go on saying the same prayers every day, then we are not growing at all. We also need to have quiet times when we can <u>listen</u> to God.

It is very easy to think we can live without God; to think that our prayers are just for when we are young and that as we grow in other ways we can forget them. It is easy to feel independent, but in reality, we need God's help for everything that we do.

A young boy once said he wasn't going to say his prayers that day, because he could not think of anything he needed. Certainly we do turn to God in times of need, but praying is much more than that. It is <u>praising God</u> (saying how wonderful and marvellous He is - a fact which we often forget); it is asking for God's forgiveness for all that we have done wrong - and we all do a great deal which is wrong, and can only feel better when we know that God, and anyone whom we have wronged, has forgiven us; it is also <u>saying 'thank-you'</u> to God for all the countless things He has given us and that He has made, for we would have nothing without God; and then it is <u>asking God</u>, both for blessings for other people and also for ourselves.

We need God in every part of life, and when we have successes and we feel good, it should never make us feel that we can do without God. We need to grow in prayer, just as we need to grow in any other part of life.

<u>A Prayer</u>:

O Lord, help us to grow in our prayer life as we grow older. May we remember to praise You, to ask Your forgiveness, to thank You, and to ask for Your blessings for other people as well as for ourselves. So may we understand how great is our need of You, and no matter what happens to us, whether it be good or bad, may we live to honour Your Name.

<u>Hymns</u>: - Father, Hear The Prayer We Offer,
'Tis Not To Ask For Gifts Alone.
Lord, Teach Us How To Pray Aright,
God Hears And Answers Prayer.

ISAAC WATTS

One day an intelligent young man complained to his father that the hymns he had heard being sung were all of very poor quality.

'Then give us something better, young man,' replied his father. Whereupon the young man sat down and began to write some splendid hymns of his own. It is said that he wrote over seven hundred hymns during his lifetime, and we have been singing them ever since, for over 250 years. He wrote hymns like *'O God, Our Help In Ages Past'*, *'When I Survey The Wondrous Cross'*, *Jesus Shall Reign Where'er The Sun'*, *'Come, Let Us Join Our Cheerful Songs'*, *'How Bright These Glorious Spirits Shine'*, and many more. The man's name was Isaac Watts.

His father was a Non-conformist (i.e. a member of another Church outside the Church of England), and at that time, Non-conformists were being persecuted because of their beliefs. Today, we do not do such things, because we know that there are many ways of worshipping God, and that it is not right to think that there is only one proper way. Isaac's father had been imprisoned for his beliefs.

When Isaac Watts wrote, *'O God, Our Help In Ages Past'*, he was probably thinking of the troublous times in which he lived. The hymn is a paraphrase *(expressing its sense in another form)* of Psalm 90 *('Lord, thou hast been our refuge: from one generation to another')*, and it has sometimes been called our country's 'second national anthem.'

When Watts was 22, he became a tutor to the family of Sir John Hartopp who lived at Stoke Newington. His next posts were as assistant pastor and then pastor of the Independent Mark Lane Chapel in the City of London. Here his fame as a preacher caused a big increase in the number of people who came to the church.

Unfortunately he did not have very good health and he had to leave his job; he went to live at the home of Sir Thomas Abney, a banker, who became Lord Mayor London in 1700.

Watts did not only write hymns; he also wrote other works on religion and was greatly interested in the work of religious education, and wrote what was probably the first children's hymn book, *'Divine and Moral Songs for Children'*.

Before his time, there were not a great many hymns in common use, and we may think of Isaac Watts as one of the founders of English hymnody.

Some men and women have always been able to put great and important truths into poetry; when set to music, and sung, they are often easier to remember than if we simply read their words. It is said that many people learn much of what they know about God through the hymns they sing; it is therefore very important that those hymns should be of excellent quality and should express the right truths. We need to choose our hymns carefully and to make sure that they say what we want to say. It is not much use singing a hymn simply because we like the tune, if the words that go with it are not good words, expressing proper truth.

Find as many hymns as you can which were written by Isaac Watts. Do you know anything about the lives of any other hymn writers? Find a name you know and, using the Index in the hymn book, find out which hymns he/she wrote; then discover what you can about his/her life. Try writing a hymn yourself.

A Prayer:
Lord God, we thank You for great writers like Isaac Watts who have given us good hymns to sing. Thank you for his ideals, his sense of excellence, and for his determination to 'write something better.' May we work equally to do our very best in all that we do.

Hymns: - Any of the hymns written by Isaac Watts, as listed in para 2 Page 57, or any other hymn which he wrote which is in the hymn book which you are using.

BEING LUKEWARM

Have you ever tried to make tea with water which was not boiling, with water which is only 'lukewarm'? It just doesn't work, does it? You can't boil an egg in it either; in fact lukewarm water is useless for that kind of job. It only achieves success when it is really boiling.

The same is true about lukewarm people, whether they are boys or girls, men or women. If you are only lukewarm about anything, then you will not get very far in that skill. You have to be boiling, red-hot keen about whatever you are doing, and then you will really achieve something.

People who run great races, or get into Premier Division football teams, or play tennis at Wimbledon, would never do so if they were only lukewarm. If they didn't much care whether they practised or not, whether they trained or not, they would never succeed. There was once a man who was very keen on his garden. Although his garden was an allotment a good distance from his home, he would get up early each morning so that he could go and weed and hoe his flower and vegetable beds before he went to work. Then in the evening, he would go back and give the plants any water or attention which they needed. If there was likely to be a sharp frost, he would go and cover up his most tender plants so that they would be sure not to die - even if it meant giving up his other hobbies to do so. People laughed at him. 'Why do you bother so much?' they asked. 'You'd still get some plants and flowers even if you didn't do all that work.'

But the man's keenness drew results. He soon had the most perfect roses and other flowers in the county. People came from miles around to look at his beautiful garden, and even consulted him about their gardening problems.

Such a person is called an enthusiast, and someone who is really keen like that is much happier and much more interesting to talk to than one who is dull and lifeless and doesn't show much interest in anything.

People who put their whole heart into something are said to have zeal and are sometimes called 'zealots'; they have energy, fervour and an eagerness to get on with whatever they are doing. They are 'boiling' people, not lukewarm people.

The people who lived in Laodicea in Bible times were anything but boiling; we are told *(Rev. 3. 14-22)* that they were neither cold not hot, they were just lukewarm - and they would not achieve much by being like that.

Lots of people have been so enthusiastic and 'boiling hot' about something - their faith, for instance - that they have died for it rather than give it up.

Are you zealous and boiling hot about your faith? About following and living in the ways you know to be right, no matter what others may say? Or do you think it doesn't much matter which way you live or what you do? Do you think you might as well do something just because 'everybody does it'? Of course it matters! If what everybody does you know to be wrong *(like taking drugs or smoking, for instance)*, then you must be red-hot keen to see that you don't follow them. It is often not very easy to stand out for what you know to be right, to be the only person not doing something or other; but this has happened in every age, and the people who stick to what they know to be right are those who really achieve something in this world.

Do you think worship is 'boring'? If so, it is probably because you are only lukewarm about it. If you put your whole heart into it, rather than just hoping it will be entertaining, then you won't find it dull or boring.

<u>A Prayer:</u>
Lord Jesus, give us a keen and zealous heart about the right and good things in life. May we put our whole heart into them, and into our worship, work and play, as though we are doing it all for You.
Thank You for keen and enthusiastic people all down the ages, who have been boiling hot for the right and have given all for You. Help us to follow their example.

<u>Hymn:</u> - Lord Of All Hopefulness
  (Note v 2 'Lord of all eagerness')
  Keep Me Shining, Lord.
  He Who Would Valiant Be.

HANDS OFF!

God had commanded the Israelites, when they went to capture the city of Jericho, that they should not take anything from the city to keep for themselves; they were not to take anything that was meant to be destroyed. If they did, it would bring trouble and destruction upon the Israelite camp. Everything that was made of silver, gold, bronze or iron was to be set apart and put in the Lord's treasury. *(Josh. 6.18-19)*. In other words, the soldiers were not to steal, for that would make them bad soldiers fighting only for what they could gain for themselves.

Now one man disobeyed this ruling. His name was Achan, and he saw a beautiful Babylonian cloak, about two kilogrammes of silver and about half a kilogramme of gold. He wanted these things so much that he stole them and went and buried them inside his tent, with the silver underneath. *(Josh. 7.20-21)*.

Because of this, the Israelites were defeated in battle. They could not expect God to be with them if they were going to disobey orders.

Joshua said the person to blame had to be found, but Achan did not own up. So Joshua had each tribe brought forward, then each clan, and then each family, until finally Achan was found out. 'It is true,' said Achan miserably. 'I sinned against God,' and he told Joshua exactly how he did it. The law in those days had a severe punishment for that kind of thief; Achan was put to death.

Now, since Jesus came to earth to show us what God is like, we have a new law. God can remove the sin from the person who has sinned - providing that person will have Jesus as his or her Saviour; this means we must repent *(be truly sorry for the sin)* and prepare to let Jesus rule our lives in the future.

Stealing is still wrong and is still punished - though people are not put to death for it these days in this country. It is a very serious matter to disobey God's laws - and 'Thou shalt not steal' was one of the Ten Commandments which God gave to Moses - but God still loves the sinner, although he hates the sin. He made rules for us and our well-being, and if everyone kept them, we should all be happy. If we break them, however, we shall suffer and we shall have to live with the punishment and the consequences. God made the world and the rules which govern it; so it stands to reason that things will only go right if they go God's way.

Your hands will do as your mind tells them, and if you see something you think you want, and it does not belong to you, your mind will say, 'Hands off!' A sensible person, who wants to obey God, will keep his hands off.

Taking something that is not yours is stealing, no matter how small the object - even if it is only a sugar lump. Lifting things from a shop is also stealing - and people do this because they think there are plenty of goods there and that no-one will notice. Nevertheless, it is still wrong and it is still stealing.

Apart from taking goods, there are other ways of stealing too. Have you ever thought that taking more than we need of anything, and so depriving someone else is stealing? If you copy the work of someone else, you are stealing their work, their thoughts and ideas. If you don't give back something you have borrowed, then that too is stealing for you are keeping what is not yours. If you don't pay bills, you are keeping the money that rightfully belongs to someone else. If you are supposed to be working, and you are perhaps reading a book under the desk, then that is stealing time. It is also stealing time when a worker does not work for his boss, but does something for himself when he is at work and should be doing the firm's work for which he is paid.

All these examples are methods of stealing. Can you think of others which we should be looking out for so that we can avoid them?

A Prayer:
Heavenly Father, we have many things to enjoy which belong to us. Help us always to remember to treat things which belong to other people properly and not to take them for our own. Help us to be careful with things which have been lent to us, and to be willing to share what we have with other people. May we always remember never to take things which are not our own.

Hymns: - Father, Lead Me Day By Day.
My Lord, My God, I Know You See.
Cleanse Me From My Sin, Lord.
Lord Of The Gentle Hands.

BELONGING

There was once a conductor of an orchestra who got very cross when the players kept missing rehearsals. One day, five of them were absent and the conductor held an inquiry the next time they all met to find out why.

The flute player said he didn't see much point in coming, as he could play his flute much better in the open air. So he had gone up into the hills to do his practising.

The man who played the triangle said he didn't feel it was worth his coming. 'I only have such a little part,' he said, 'and I can do it just as well at home.'

One of the second violins said, 'Mine isn't a big part either; the first violins are much more important, and anyway there are quite a lot of us violinists, so I thought you'd never miss me.'

The conductor was getting more and more angry. 'And what about you?' he said to the man who played the big bass drum and who thought rather a lot of himself.

'I felt I'd no need,' replied the drummer. 'I know my part well, and I'm as good as those who do go to rehearsal - in fact, better than most.'

The cellist was more modest. 'I'm not much good at my part,' he said. 'All those low notes, you know. I never feel I get much out of it when I do go to rehearsal, so I thought I'd stay at home.'

The conductor got very red in the face. 'Don't you know,' he thundered, 'that _all_ the parts are important, however small you may think them. We are all there to help one another, and it is your duty to come, whether you feel like it or not. You have to think of the other players. The fact that _you_ don't feel you get anything out of it does not matter at all. What _does_ matter is what you put into it, for the sake of the other players and for the sake of the whole sound. If ever any one of you is absent, it spoils the whole piece of music. It just doesn't sound right - even though there is only one part missing. You are all important and you all have your part to play - and no-one else can do it for you.'

If we belong to something, say the Church, then it is up to us to go regularly and to do our part. You would not think much of a boy who said he was a scout but who hardly ever went to the meetings. The same is true of a Christian.

Belonging to things is a very important part of life. We cannot be very happy if we try to exist all on our own. Have you ever noticed a coal fire, which is made up of lots of separate pieces of coal? When they are all in the grate together, they burn up fiercely and well. However, if one coal falls out on to the hearth, it will not go on burning for very long; soon it will die down and finally it will go completely dead - because it is not with the others. One on its own soon flickers and dies, but all the coals together can make a good fire and a big glow.

If we all go to an organisation, it will encourage others. But if we only go now and then, when we feel like it, then people will think that it cannot be much of an organisation if we are as haphazard as that. So we shall be letting down the whole organisation. This is very true of the Church. One Christian on his own is not likely to be very encouraging to others - although one person can indeed do great things for God. But far better things and greater things can be done by a group banded together - in other words, the local church. We make various excuses not to go, just like the players in the orchestra, but in the end, we must see that we each have our part to play and that no-one else can do it for us.

<u>A Prayer</u>:

Lord Jesus Christ, it is right to belong to a good organisation and especially to be a member of your Church - the body of Christian people who have loved and followed You down the ages. Help me to be a regular, helpful member, and to play my part in helping the good to go forward in life, so that I may do my bit to help the world to become a happier place and to worship You.

<u>Hymns</u>: - Thy Hand, O God, Has Guided
We Love The Place, O God
There Are Hundreds Of Sparrows.

WHAT YOU ARE REALLY LIKE

One day a lady customer went into the village shop. The shop was kept by a little old lady who was rather dumpy and didn't move about too easily. The customer wanted some sweets which were kept in a jar on the top shelf behind the counter.

The shopkeeper looked rather worried. 'I'm afraid I can't reach the jar myself, and I can no longer climb ladders,' she said. 'If you would not mind waiting, my husband will be back shortly and he will get the jar down for you.'

'Of course, I don't mind waiting,' said the customer, and she stood back. Behind her was a very rough-looking youth, waiting his turn to be served. He looked untidy and dirty and had a shock of unkempt hair. The lady customer felt rather afraid of him, for she never quite trusted rough-looking people these days, since one had crashed into her garden wall on his motor bike, and had ridden off, apparently unhurt, without even saying he was sorry, nor offering to help to repair the damage.

To her surprise however, the youth in the shop stepped forward with a bright smile.

'I'm quite tall,' he said. 'Perhaps I could get the jar down for you and then this lady will not have to wait.'

The surprised shopkeeper said, 'Thank you very much,' and the boy reached down the jar, waited while she weighed out the sweets and then he put the jar back for her.

The shopkeeper thanked him again and then served him with the bar of chocolate for which he was waiting.

When he had gone out, the shopkeeper turned to the lady customer and said, 'Now that has taught me a lesson. I've always rather looked down on dirty, scruffy-looking people, but it seems they can be as nice and helpful as anyone else.'

The customer agreed. 'That boy had better manners and acted more thoughtfully that some of the cleanest-looking and well-dressed people I know.' she said. 'I'm beginning to understand that you can't always judge by what a person looks like on the outside. It's the person inside the clothes who really matters.'

We may think that we prefer clean, tidy, decent-looking

people, but we must remember that what they <u>are</u> is more important than how they look.

Sometimes we put on what we call a 'front', when we act and say things which we don't really mean, but which we think are the sort of things people expect of us. Can you think of times when this happens? Can you think of times when you have judged a person just because of the way he or she looks, without troubling to find out what that person was really like?

The boy in the story felt happier than he had done for a long time, for he had had a chance to prove what he really was - even if only in a small way. He felt no-one had really bothered about him before, and that they had simply looked down on him because of the way he dressed.

In some cases, people who are ugly or who may perhaps have a scar are not treated well by people who tend to avoid them. We should always remember that what a person <u>is</u> is much more important than how he looks. God always sees the insides of us - the real us - and he knows exactly the kind of people we are.

How do you think people see you? How do you think God sees you?

<u>A Prayer</u>:
Lord Jesus, help us never to despise people just because of the way they look; help us rather to try and find out what the real person is like, so that we may give them the chance to show us what they really are. May we try and show forth the real good in us, and not feel that the outside appearance can help us to get by when our behaviour is not of the best. Help us to remember that You see us as we really are.

<u>Hymns</u> - Blest Are The Pure In Heart
Fill Thou My Life, O Lord My God
There's A Fight To Be Fought

SYMBOLS IN ROAD SIGNS

(If possible a chart, displaying various road signs, should be put up for this assembly).

Do you cycle? Have you passed your cycling proficiency test? If so, then you must have learnt the Highway Code and must know what the various signs mean. Perhaps you recognise the ones shown on this chart? If you are a cyclist, I hope you do!

These signs can also help us to remember how to live our lives; you can think of them as God's signs on the road through life.

For instance, <u>STOP</u> could remind you to stop when you are intending to do something which you know to be wrong.

a <u>An arrow</u>, <u>pointing to the right</u>, could tell you to turn to the right way of doing something, and to follow the way which you know to be right.

<u>GIVE WAY</u> - When you want something, and it is selfish of you to want it, then this sign can remind you that it is right to give way to other people. Even in little things, when there is a crowd or a queue, you must remember to give way to other people before yourself.

<u>ONE WAY</u> can remind you that there is only one way to live and that is God's way. He made the world and things will only go right if they go His way.

You don't have to be a cyclist or even a motorist to take note of these signs. Even if you are just walking along the street, you can be reminded of the things of God when you see the road signs.

The <u>traffic signals</u> themselves - red, amber and green, can remind us that God has <u>three</u> answers to prayer. Sometimes we say we have prayed for something and that God has not answered us if we have not received it. God <u>has</u> certainly answered our prayers, but it may not always be in the way we expect.

God alone really knows what is best for us, and sometimes our answer is like the <u>red</u> traffic light. It says '<u>No</u>' for God knows that the thing for which we are asking is not good for us; therefore He does not grant our prayer. Just as mother would not go on giving us chocolates and chips if we kept on asking for she would know that to go on eating such things would make us ill.

Sometimes God's answer is like the <u>amber</u> traffic light, which says 'Wait '. This is when God knows that the time is not right for us to have what we have prayed for. The important thing is to remember that God knows best and that the right will win in the end, and to go on trusting him.

When God answers our prayer in the way we want - as He does if it is right for us, - then that answer is 'Yes' and is like the <u>green</u> traffic light.

The road signs and traffic lights which we have been talking about can be looked on as simple reminders about the way we live our lives. If you are to be a Christian, that is a follower of Jesus Christ, then you will want to live His way, which is God's way. This does not mean only going to church and saying your prayers and thinking that that is all that it is necessary to do. No, it means living the way Jesus wants us to live all through the week, on Monday, Tuesday, Wednesday, Thursday, Friday and Saturday, as well as Sunday. For to do the job properly affects our whole lives. The signs in the roads are just one of the sorts of things which can remind us what our life is supposed to be. Can you think of any other signs which will be a help in this kind of way?

(NB: Be careful not to be thinking too much about the 'other meanings' of the road signs, when you should be concentrating on the traffic!)

<u>A Prayer</u>:
> *Lord Jesus, help us to live our lives in Your way. Help us to stop doing wrong and to turn to the right way of doing things. Help us to put other people before ourselves, to give way, and not to be selfish; and may we remember that there is only one way to live if we want to be truly happy and that is Your Way.*

<u>Hymns</u> - Children Of The Heavenly King
              Oft In Danger, Oft In Woe
              Loving Shepherd Of Thy Sheep
              Father, Lead Me Day By Day

I BELIEVE

One cold freezing January day, two boys went for a walk in the park. When they came to the pond, they found that it was covered over with ice. This meant they could not see if there were any fish in it or not, and that is what they had wanted to see.

'I think we could see through the ice if we went into the middle of the pond,' said Tim. 'The ice is clearer there and it doesn't look as though it is so thickly covered with frost.'

Tom looked hard at the surface. 'But I think the ice is thinner there,' he said, 'so it will not be safe to walk on it.'

'Nonsense,' said Tim. 'It has been freezing for days now, and the ice will be as thick as thick. It's nearly solid on the bird bath at home. Anyway, I believe it is quite safe all the way in, and I'm going to walk to the middle to show you.'

So Tim set off, walking carefully at first, and Tom watched anxiously from the bank. Suddenly there was a loud crack, followed by a loud yell from Tim. The ice had cracked and Tim was spluttering in the freezing cold water. Quickly Tom ran to some nearby adults and asked for their help; one of the men went and brought a ladder, and in the end, they were able to drag a wet and bedraggled Tim out on to the bank.

'But I believed it was safe! I really did!' he kept saying. 'I would not have gone if I hadn't believed it was thick enough to hold me!'

'Perhaps you didn't notice that sign saying 'Danger! Thin ice!' suggested one of the men.

'Well, I did,' admitted Tim, 'but I thought it would hold me. I really believed it would!'

If Tim had not believed the ice was strong enough to hold

him, he would never have ventured into the middle. What we <u>do</u> depends on what we <u>believe</u>. If we believe the right things, we will do the right things. <u>Right actions depend on right beliefs</u>.

But if we believe the wrong things, then we will do the wrong things.

When the Church began after Jesus had gone back to heaven, it had lots of enemies, people who attacked the Faith and who twisted it and misrepresented it. So there had to be some definite statement of what they believed, something which all the people who wanted to follow Jesus's religion and way of life would know were the things to believe in. So a <u>creed</u> was drawn up. A creed is a summary of the things which (in this case) a Christian ought to know and believe. Creeds are like the colours or flags which are carried at the head of an army. They mean something of great value and they tell us the things which we must stand up and defend. Can you think of other things in which what we do depends on what we believe?

<u>A Prayer:</u>

Lord Jesus, help me to believe what is true and right, so that I may take the right actions and say the right things in life. Help me to know that if I believe the right things, then it will help me to do the right things, and so will give me a standard to guide me in life's journey.

<u>Hymns</u>   -   O God of Faith, Help Me Believe.
             Firmly I Believe and Truly.

QUARRELS AND ARGUMENTS

Do you know the Shakespeare play 'Romeo and Juliet'? In it there are two great families, the Montague's and the Capulet's. Long ago, these two families had quarrelled, and though most people had forgotten what the quarrel was about, they just could not forget that there had been a quarrel and that they must therefore always be enemies with each other. So the Montagues wouldn't speak to the Capulets and the Capulets wouldn't speak to the Montagues - or if they did, it was only to say something rude and unkind. Often this ended in a fight. Their relations and servants were just as bad, and the quarrel went on for years and years, without most of the people having any idea what it was all about and why they were behaving in such a silly way. Romeo was a young Montague and Juliet was the daughter of Lord Capulet, and when they fell in love and wanted to get married, it caused all sorts of trouble.

You will probably be thinking how silly it all was, and that real people don't behave like the Montagues and Capulets. But they do. Even today, over fifty years after the end of the 2nd World War, you will still get people saying they hate all the people who were on the other side, and that they would not speak to one of them if they met them! Isn't it silly? There are very many very good people on both sides, and we have to learn to forget the past and to see one another as friends.

Do you ever say you're not playing with so-and-so ever again because of something they did which you didn't like? Isn't that just as silly? It is also wrong. The proper thing to do is to forget the wrong, forgive the other person and be friends again. This is not at all easy to do, but it is the right thing to do, and if we can do it, we will find we are much happier people. If you let wrongs fester inside you, they only grow and get worse and worse.

It is easy to be good and kind to those who agree with you. It is not so easy to behave well towards those with whom you have quarrelled. But that is the way God wants us to live - being kind and forgiving to those who have quarrelled with us - and remembering that they may be in the right.

This question of how long he should put up with someone who disagreed with him troubled St Peter in the Bible. One day he went to Jesus and asked, 'Lord, how often shall I forgive someone who keeps sinning against me? Seven times?'

Peter no doubt thought he was being very good to forgive someone seven times; but Jesus's answer surprised him.

'Not seven times,' said Jesus, 'but seventy times seven.' In other words, for ever. *(Matthew 18. 21-22)*. We must go on forgiving people all through life. We need God's help to do anything as difficult as this, but if we ask Him for it, and trust Him to give it, then He will surely help us to be forgiving people. It is not a lesson we can learn all at once, but we can go on getting better at it as we go through life.

A Prayer:
Dear Lord Jesus, help us to be more friendly towards one another, to speak gently and to act kindly. Teach us to forgive and forget when someone has wronged us, and help us to try and see their point of view.
Forgive us for the times when we have done and said wrong things and have been unkind to others; and help us to be friendly and forgiving people now and always.

Hymns - Father, Hear The Prayer We Offer
              Lord Of All Hopefulness, Lord Of All Joy
              Heavenly Father, May Thy Blessing

MOORLEY'S are growing Publishers, adding several new titles to our list each year. We also undertake private publications and commissioned works.

Our range of publications includes: **Books of Verse**
- Devotional Poetry
- Recitations

Drama
- Bible Plays
- Sketches
- Nativity Plays
- Passiontide Plays
- Easter Plays
- Demonstrations

Resource Books
- Assembly Material
- Songs & Musicals
- Children's Addresses
- Prayers & Graces
- Daily Readings
- Books for Speakers

Activity Books
- Quizzes
- Puzzles
- Painting Books

Daily Readings

Church Stationery
- Notice Books
- Cradle Rolls
- Hymn Board Numbers

Please send a S.A.E. (approx 9" x 6") for the current catalogue or consult your local Christian Bookshop who should stock or be able to order our titles.